QUICK LANGUAGES

MULTI-LANGUAGE PHRASEBOOK COLLECTION

AMERICAN
BOOK GROUP

ENGLISH-JAPANESE
JAPANESE-ENGLISH

GET THE AUDIOVISUAL AND
INTERACTIVE CONTENT AT
QuickLanguages.com

QUICK LANGUAGES

MULTI-LANGUAGE PHRASEBOOK COLLECTION

SPEAK ANY LANGUAGE NOW!

WHAT IS QUICK LANGUAGES?

Did you know that we only use about 1,000 words in our everyday vocabulary? The same goes for any language! So, mastering a digital phrasebook with interactive pronunciation tools is a smart alternative to long and expensive language instruction.

Quick Languages is an interactive phrasebook that introduces you to the 12 predominant world languages all in one convenient drop-down menu. Designed for visual, auditory, and kinesthetic learners alike, it is simple, affordable, and effective.

Own the potential of connecting with over 3 billion people!

GET THE AUDIOVISUAL AND INTERACTIVE CONTENT AT
QuickLanguages.com

QUICK LANGUAGES

MULTI-LANGUAGE PHRASEBOOK COLLECTION

SPEAK ANY LANGUAGE NOW!

QUICK LANGUAGES PHRASEBOOK COLLECTION
AVAILABLE TITLES

1. ENGLISH-SPANISH & SPANISH-ENGLISH
2. ENGLISH-ITALIAN & ITALIAN-ENGLISH
3. ENGLISH-FRENCH & FRENCH-ENGLISH
4. ENGLISH-GERMAN & GERMAN-ENGLISH
5. ENGLISH-PORTUGUESE & PORTUGUESE-ENGLISH
6. ENGLISH-CHINESE & CHINESE-ENGLISH
7. ENGLISH-ARABIC & ARABIC-ENGLISH
8. ENGLISH-JAPANESE & JAPANESE-ENGLISH
9. ENGLISH-KOREAN & KOREAN-ENGLISH
10. ENGLISH-RUSSIAN & RUSSIAN-ENGLISH
11. ENGLISH-TURKISH & TURKISH-ENGLISH

AMERICAN
BOOK GROUP

COMPANION ONLINE COURSE
quicklanguages.com

Quick Languages: 1,000 Key Words and Expressions Phrasebook
ENGLISH-JAPANESE & JAPANESE-ENGLISH

To request permissions, contact the publisher at info@trialtea.com

Paperback ISBN: 978-1-681656-17-5

Library of Congress Control Code: 2023932197

First paperback edition: April 2023

Edited by Gregorio García
Cover art by Natalia Urbano
Layout by Esmeralda Riveros & Pancho Guijarro

Printed in the USA

American Book Group
americanbookgroup.com

Quick Languages / 1,000 Key Words and Phrases

INDEX OF CONTENTS

1,000 KEY WORDS AND EXPRESSIONS

English / Japanese - Japanese / English

1. Greetings / 挨拶

Hi! / Hello!	こんにちは / やぁ!
Good morning	おはようございます
Good afternoon	こんにちは / やぁ!
Good evening / Good night	こんばんは
How are you doing?	元気ですか？ / ご機嫌いかがですか？
Fine	元気です
Very well	とても元気です
Thank you / Thanks	ありがとう
Thank you very much	どうもありがとう
You're welcome	どういたしまして
Fine, thank you	元気です、ありがとう
And you?	君は（のほうは元気）？
See you	またね
See you later	また後で
See you tomorrow	また明日
Goodbye	さようなら
Bye	バイバイ、じゃぁね

2. Introductions and Courtesy Expressions /
自己紹介と挨拶表現

English	Japanese
What is your name?	あなたのお名前は？
My name is ...	私の名前は・・・
Who are you?	どなたですか？
I am ...	私は・・・
Who is he / she?	彼 (el)/彼女(ella) は誰ですか？
He is ... / She is ...	彼(el) / 彼女(ella) は・・・
Nice to meet you / Pleased to meet you	お会いできて光栄です
Nice to meet you, too	こちらこそ、お会いできて光栄です
It's my pleasure	光栄です
Excuse me	すみません
Please	お願いします / ～して下さい
One moment, please	少しお待ちください
Welcome	ようこそ
Go ahead	お入りください
Can you repeat, please?	もう一度、繰り返して下さい
I don't understand	分かりません
I understand a little	少し理解できます
Can you speak more slowly, please?	ゆっくり話してくれませんか？
Do you speak Spanish?	スペイン語を話しますか？
How do you say hello in Spanish?	ハロー(hello)はスペイン語で何と言いますか？
What does it mean?	これは何という意味ですか？
I speak Spanish a little	私は少しスペイン語を話します。

3. Ways to Address to a Person / 人の呼び方

Madam / Ma'am	（既婚）～さん、夫人
Miss	（未婚）～さん、～嬢
Ms.	～さん
Mr.	（男性）～さん、～氏
Mrs.	（既婚）女性
Sir	男性
Dr.	博士

4. The Articles / 冠詞

The	∅
The car	自動車
The cars	自動車（複数形）
The house	家
The houses	家（複数形）
A	
A car	自動車
A house	家
An	∅
An elephant	象
An apple	リンゴ
Some	いくつかの
Some cars	自動車（複数形）
Some houses	家（複数形）

5. The Subject Pronouns / 人称代名詞

I	私
You	君 / あなた
He	彼
She	彼女
It	彼たち、彼ら
We	私たち
You	あなたたち
They	彼ら / 彼女ら

6. The Possessive Adjectives / 属格

My	私の
Your	君の
His	彼の
Her	彼女の
Its	彼らの
Our	私たちの
Your	君たちの
Their	彼たちの / 彼女たちの
My car	私の自動車
Your book	君の本
His TV	彼のテレビ
Our house	私たちの家

7. The Demonstrative Adjectives / 指示詞

This	この
This book	この本
This shirt	このシャツ
These	これらの
These books	これらの本
These shirts	これらのシャツ
That	その
That table	そのテーブル
That car	その自動車
Those	それらの
Those tables	それらのテーブル
Those cars	それらの自動車

8. The Possessive Pronouns / 所有格

Mine	私の
Yours	君の
His	彼の
Hers	彼女の
Its	彼の
Ours	私たちの
Yours	君たちの
Theirs	彼 / 彼女たちの
The car is mine	自動車は私のです
The book is yours	本は君のです
That TV is his	そのテレビは彼女のです
This house is ours	この家は私たちのです

9. The Cardinal Numbers /
基本数字

0 / Zero	0 零
1 / One	1 一
2 / Two	2 二
3 / Three	3 三
4 / Four	4 四
5 / Five	5 五
6 / Six	6 六
7 / Seven	7 七
8 / Eight	8 八
9 / Nine	9 九
10 / Ten	10 十
11 / Eleven	11 十一
12 / Twelve	12 十二
13 / Thirteen	13 十三
14 / Fourteen	14 十四
15 / Fifteen	15 十五
16 / Sixteen	16 十六
17 / Seventeen	17 十七
18 / Eighteen	18 十八
19 / Nineteen	19 十九
20 / Twenty	20 二十
21 / Twenty-one	21 二十一
30 / Thirty	30 三十
40 / Forty	40 四十
50 / Fifty	50 五十
60 / Sixty	60 六十

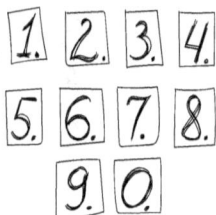

9. The Cardinal Numbers / 基本数字

70 / Seventy	70	七十
80 / Eighty	80	八十
90 /Ninety	90	九十
100 / One hundred	100	百
101 / One hundred and one	101	百一
200 / Two hundred	200	二百
300 / Three hundred	300	三百
400 / Four hundred	400	四百
500 / Five hundred	500	五百
600 / Six hundred	600	六百
700 / Seven hundred	700	七百
800 / Eight hundred	800	八百
900 /Nine hundred	900	九百
1,000 / One thousand	1000	千
10,000 / Ten thousand	10000	一万
100,000 / One hundred thousand	100000	十万
1,000,000 / One million	1000000	百万
1,000,000,000 / One billion	1000000000	十億
Forty-five (45)	45	四十五
One hundred and twenty-eight (128)	128	百二十八
One thousand nine hundred and sixty-three (1,963)	1963	千九百六十三
Six thousand and thirty-seven (6,037)	6037	六千三十七
Eleven thousand (11,000)	11000	一万千
Two hundred and seventy-nine thousand (279,000)	279000	二十七万九千
Two million (2,000,000)	2000000	二百万

10. The Time /
時間

The clock	時計
The watch	腕時計
What time is it?	何時ですか？
It is ...	・・・時です
It is one o'clock (1:00)	1時です
It is two o'clock (2:00)	2時です
It is three fifteen / It is a quarter past three (3:15)	3時15分です
It is four thirty / It is half past four (4:30)	4時30分です / 4時半です
It is five forty-five / It is a quarter to six (5:45)	5時45分です / 6時15分前です
It is six fifty / It is ten to seven (6:50)	6時50分です / 7時10分前です
It is noon (12:00 P. M.)	正午です
It is midnight (12:00 A. M.)	真夜中 / 午前零時
In the morning	午前中に
In the afternoon	午後に
In the evening	夜に
At night	夜に
At what time is ...?	・・・は何時ですか？
At what time is the concert?	コンサートは何時ですか？
At ...	・・・時に
At 7:10 P.M. (seven ten in the evening)	夜7時に

11. The Days of the Week / 曜日

Monday	月曜日
Tuesday	火曜日
Wednesday	水曜日
Thursday	木曜日
Friday	金曜日
Saturday	土曜日
Sunday	日曜日
What day is today?	今日は何曜日ですか？

12. The Months of the Year / 月

January	一月
February	二月
March	三月
April	四月
May	五月
June	六月
July	七月
August	八月
September	九月
October	十月
November	十一月
December	十二月
What is today's date?	今日は何日ですか？

13. The Weather / 気候

Sunny	晴れ
Cloudy	曇り
Rainy	雨がちの
Humid	じめじめした
Dry	乾燥した
Cold	寒い
Warm	暑い
Hot	暑い
Rain	雨
Snow	雪
How is the weather today?	今日の天気はどうですか？
It's nice	いい天気です
It's sunny	晴れています
It's cold in winter	冬は寒いです
It's raining	雨が降っています
It's snowing	雪が降っています
I am cold	（私は）寒いです

14. The Seasons / 季節

Spring	春
Summer	夏
Fall	秋
Winter	冬

15. The Colors / 色

Yellow	黄色
Red	赤
Blue	青
Green	緑
Orange	オレンジ色
Brown	茶色
Pink	ピンク色
Purple	赤紫色
Black	黒
White	白
Gray	灰色
Light	明るい
Dark	暗い
Light green	明るい緑（黄緑）
Orange book	オレンジ色の本
Brown shoes	茶色い靴
My blouse is white	私のブラウスは白です
What color is...?	・・・は何色ですか？
What is your favorite color?	君の好きな色は何ですか？

16. The Parts of the Face / 顔の部分

Cheek	頬
Chin	顎
Ear	耳
Eye	目
Forehead	おでこ
Hair	髪
Lips	唇
Mouth	口
Nose	鼻
Skin	皮膚
Teeth	歯（複数形）
Tooth	歯
Blond / Blonde	金髪の
Brown	栗毛の
Gray	白髪の
Red hair	赤毛の
Long	長い
Short	短い
Straight	直毛の
Curly	巻毛の
John is blond	ジョンは金髪です
Karen has long hair	カレンは髪が長いです
He has green eyes	彼は緑目です
Her eyes are blue	彼の目は青いです
His eyes are big and brown	彼の目は大きくて茶色です

17. Essential Verbs /
基本動詞

English	Japanese
Be	～である
Go	行く
Come	来る
Have	持つ
Get	達成する、獲得する
Help	助ける、手伝う
Love	愛する
Like	気に入る
Want	欲する；望む、願う
Buy	買う
Sell	売る
Read	読む
Write	書く
Drink	飲む
Eat	食べる
Open	開く、開ける
Close	閉める、閉じる
Look at	見る
Look for	探す
Find	見つける
Start	始める
Stop	止める
Pull	引っ張る

17. Essential Verbs /
基本動詞

Push	押す
Send	送る
Receive	受け取る
Turn on	点火する；スイッチを入れる
Turn off	消す
Listen to	聞く
Speak	話す
Do	する
Drive	操る；操作する
Feel	感じる
Know	知っている
Leave	出る
Live	生きる；住む
Make	準備する
Meet	知り合う
Need	必要とする
Pay	払う
Play	遊ぶ
Remember	思い出す / 覚えている
Repeat	繰り返す
Say	言う
Sit	座る
Sleep	寝る

17. Essential Verbs / 基本動詞

Study	勉強する
Take	取る、つかむ
Think	考える
Understand	理解する
Wait	待つ
Watch	観察する
There is	ある
There are	ある
I am tall	私は（背が）高いです
You are short	君は（背が）小さいです
He is thin	彼は痩せています
We are big	私たちは大きいです
They are intelligent	彼らは頭が良いです
I am at home	私は家に居ます
You are at school	君は学校にいます
We are at the store	私たちはお店にいます
I get a prize	私は賞を取ります
I go to the movies	私は映画館に行きます
I have a nice car	私は素敵な自動車を持っています
I listen to the music	私は音楽を聞きます
I watch TV.	私はテレビを観ます
I like this book	私はこの本が好きです
There are ten children in the park	公園に10人の子供がいます

18. Interrogative Words /
疑問文

How many ...?	いくつの（複数形）・・・？
How much...?	いくつの（単数形）・・・？
How ...?	どのように？
What ...?	何？
When ...?	いつ？
Where ...?	どこで？
Which ...?	どれ？
Who ...?	誰？
Whose ...?	誰の？
Whom ...? / To whom ...?	誰に？
Why ...?	なぜ？
Because ...	なぜなら・・・

19. Linking Words /
接続詞

And	・・・と
But	しかし、でも・・・
Or	または
Either ... or	・・・か・・・か
Neither ... nor	・・・も・・・もない
Yes	はい
No	いいえ
So	それでは
While	・・・している間

20. The Prepositions / 前置詞

About	～について
Above	～の上に
Across	～の前に
At	～に
Behind	～の後ろに
Below	～の下に
Between	～の間に
By	～で〔交通手段〕
Down	下方に
During	～の間に〔時間・期間〕
For	～のために
From	～から
In	～の中に
In front of	～の正面に
Into	中に

20. The Prepositions /
前置詞

Near	近くに
Next to	～の隣に
Of	～の
On	～の上に
Out	外に
Over	～の上に
Per	～で、～のゆえに
Through	～を通して
To	～の方へ
Under	下に
Up	上に
With	～と一緒に
Without	～なしに
The cat is in the box	箱の中に猫がいます
The vase is on the table	テーブルの上に花瓶があります
Somebody is at the door	玄関に誰か居ます

21. Giving Directions / 道案内

At the corner	角に
Far	遠くに
Near	近くに
Go straight ahead	まっすぐ進んでください
Left	左
Right	右
Turn left	左に曲がる
Turn right	右に曲がる
Go straight one block	1 街区 (ブロック) まっすぐ進んでください
After the traffic light, turn right	信号の後で右に曲がる
How can I get to ...?	・・・へはどのように行けばいいですか？
Where is the ...?	・・・はどこですか？
Where is the church?	教会はどこですか？
The museum is next to the shopping center	美術館はショッピングセンターの隣です。
The drugstore is in front of the building	薬局はビルの前です。
The supermarket is near the park	スーパーマーケットは公園の近くです。

22. The Ordinal Numbers / 序数

First	最初の、第1の
Second	2番目の、第2の
Third	3番目の、第3の
Fourth	4番目の、第4の
Fifth	5番目の、第5の
Sixth	6番目の、第6の
Seventh	7番目の、第7の
Eighth	8番目の、第8の
Ninth	9番目の、第9の
Tenth	10番目の、第10の
Eleventh	11番目の、第11の
Twelfth	12番目の、第12の
Twentieth	20番目の；20分の1
Thirtieth	30番目の；30分の1
The first building	最初の建物
The second floor	1階

23. Countries, Nationalities, and Languages / 国・国籍・言語

Brazil (Country)	ブラジル (国)
Brazilian (Nationality)	ブラジル人 (国籍)
Portuguese (Language)	ポルトガル語 (言語)
Colombia	コロンビア
Colombian	コロンビア人
Spanish	スペイン語
China	中国
Chinese	中国人
Chinese	中国語
England	イギリス
English	イギリス人
English	英語
France	フランス
French	フランス人
French	フランス語
Germany	ドイツ
German	ドイツ人
German	ドイツ語
Italy	イタリア

23. Countries, Nationalities, and Languages /
国・国籍・言語

Italian	イタリア人
Italian	イタリア語
Japan	日本
Japanese	日本人
Japanese	日本語
Mexico	メキシコ
Mexican	メキシコ人
Spanish	スペイン語
Spain	スペイン
Spanish	スペイン人
Spanish	スペイン語
United States of America (U.S.A.)	アメリカ合衆国
American	アメリカ人
English	英語
Where are you from?	どこの出身ですか？
I am from Brazil	私はブラジル出身です。
I am Brazilian	私はブラジル人です。
I speak Portuguese	私はポルトガル語を話します。
I am not from Italy	私はイタリア出身ではありません。

24. Indefinite Pronouns / 不定代名詞

Anybody	誰か（疑問）、誰も（否定）
Anything	何か（疑問）、何も（否定）
Nobody	誰も
Nothing	何も
Somebody	誰か（肯定）
Something	何か（肯定）
Everybody	全部（複数形）、すべて
Everything	全部、すべて
Is anybody home?	どなたか家に居ますか？
I don't want anything	何もいらない
Nothing happened	なんでもない
Somebody is in the living room	応接間に誰かいる
Everything is ready	準備万端

25. The Emotions /
感情

Angry	怒った
Bored	つまらない
Confident	自信を持った
Confused	混乱した
Embarrassed	恥じている
Excited	熱狂した
Happy	満足した
Nervous	緊張した
Proud	誇り高い
Sad	悲しい
Scared	怖がらせた
Shy	内気な
Surprised	驚いた
Worried	心配させた
I am happy	（私は）満足しています
He is sad	彼は悲しんでいます
They are surprised	彼らは驚いています
Are you excited?	あなたは興奮(熱狂)していますか？
I am not bored	（私は）退屈していません
She is not nervous	彼女は緊張していません
Everybody is confident	すべての人は自信を持っています

26. Adverbs / 副詞

A few	少しの
A little	わずかな
A lot	たくさんの
After	後で
Again	もう一度
Ago	後ろへ
Also	・・・もまた
Always	いつも
Before	前に、以前に
Enough	十分に
Everyday	毎日
Exactly	正確に
Finally	最後に
First	まず最初に
Here	ここ
Late	遅く、遅れて
Later	もっと遅く
Never	決して（・・・ない）
Next	次の、近い
Now	今

26. Adverbs /
副詞

Often	しょっちゅう
Once	一回
Only	・・・だけ、ただ・・・
Outside	外へ
Really	現実に、本当に
Right here	ちょうど此処
Right now	今すぐに
Since	・・・から
Slowly	ゆっくりと
Sometimes	時々、たまに
Soon	すぐに
Still	まだ（・・・ない）
Then	後で
There	あちらの方へ
Today	今日
Tomorrow	明日
Tonight	今晩
Too	・・・もまた
Usually	通常、ふつう

27. Auxiliary Verbs / 助動詞

Can	・・・できる
Could	・・・してくれませんか
Did	・・・できた
Do	する
Does	する
Have to	・・・しなければならない
May	・・・しても良い
Must	・・・しなければならない
Should	・・・したほうが良い
Will	∅
Would	∅
Can you go to the movies?	映画を観にいける？
Could I have change?	両替していただけますか？
Did you work at the drugstore?	（君は）薬局で働いていた？
I did not (didn't) work at the drugstore	（私は）薬局では働いていませんでした。
Do you work at the drugstore?	（君は）薬局で働いている？
I do not (don't) work at the drugstore	（私は）薬局では働いていません。
Does he read the newspaper?	彼は新聞を読みますか？
He does not (doesn't) read the newspaper	彼は新聞を読みません。
I have to do my homework	（私は）自分の仕事をしなければなりません。
May I help you?	何かお手伝いできますか？
You must turn left now	（君は）今、左に曲がるべきだ。
You should go to the doctor	（君は）医者に行くべきだ。
I will work tomorrow	（私は）明日働きます。
I would like a glass of wine	（私は）ワイン一杯いただけますか？

28. Expressions /
表現

All right	それで良い
Come in	どうぞ
Come here, please	こちらに来てください。
Don't worry!	心配いらないよ！
For example	例えば・・・
Good luck!	幸運を！
Great idea!	グッド・アイディア！
Have a nice day!	良い一日を（過ごしてください）！
Help yourself!	どうぞご自由に！/ セルフサービスです！
Here you are	どうぞ
Hurry up!	急いで！
I agree	賛同する、賛成する
I disagree	私は反対です
I don't care	私はどちらでもいいです
I don't know	知りません
I'm coming!	今、行きます！
I'm afraid...	・・・ではないかと心配する
It's a deal!	約束したぞ！/ 話しは決まった！
Keep well!	ごきげんよう
Let me think	考えさせてください
Let's go!	さあ！/ さあ行こう！
Right now	たった今 / 現在
Sounds good!	いいね
Sure	確かに
Take a seat	お座りください
Take care!	気をつけて！

29. The Family / 家族

Father	父
Mother	母
Son	息子
Daughter	娘
Brother	兄弟
Sister	姉妹
Grandfather	祖父
Grandmother	祖母
Uncle	伯父・叔父
Aunt	伯母・叔母
Cousin	いとこ
Nephew	甥
Niece	姪
Husband	夫
Wife	妻
Boyfriend	彼氏 / 新郎
Girlfriend	彼女 / 新婦
In-laws	義理の家族
Father in-law	義父・舅
Mother in-law	義母・姑
Brother in-law	義兄・義弟
Sister in-law	義姉・義妹
Step father	継父
Step mother	継母
Step brother	異父（異母）の兄弟
Step sister	異父（異母）の姉妹
Who is he?	彼は誰ですか？
He is my brother	彼は私の兄（弟）です。

30. The House /
家

Living room	応接間
Door	ドア・扉
Window	窓
Sofa	ソファ
Lamp	ランプ
Dining room	食堂
Table	テーブル / 机
Chair	椅子
Kitchen	台所 / キッチン
Stove	ストーブ
Oven	オーブン
Fridge	冷蔵庫
Microwave	電子レンジ
Bedroom	寝室
Bed	ベッド
Nightstand	ナイトテーブル
Vanity	鏡台
Chest of drawers	整理だんす
Closet	クローゼット
Bathroom	浴室
Mirror	鏡
Sink	洗面台 / 洗面所
Toilet	水洗トイレ
Bathtub	浴槽
Laundry room	コインランドリー
Driveway	駐車場
Where is the living room?	応接室はどこですか？
The door is big	ドアは大きいです。
The stove is small	ストーブは小さいです。
The kitchen is beautiful	キッチンは素敵です。

31. The City /
街

Block	街区 / ブロック
Building	ビル / 建物
Church	教会
Movie theater	映画館
Museum	美術館 / 博物館
Park	公園
Drugstore	薬局
Restaurant	レストラン
Shopping center	ショッピングセンター
Store	店
Street	道
Supermarket	スーパーマーケット

32. At the Supermarket / スーパーマーケットで

The food	食品
The fruits	果物
Apple	リンゴ
Banana	バナナ
Cherry	さくらんぼ
Grapes	ブドウ
Orange	オレンジ
Strawberry	苺
The vegetables	野菜
Beans	インゲン豆
Carrot	人参
Cauliflower	カリフラワー
Lettuce	レタス
Onion	玉ねぎ
Pepper	ピーマン
Potato	ジャガイモ
Tomato	トマト
The meats	肉
Beef	牛肉
Chicken	鶏肉
Turkey	七面鳥
Ham	生ハム
Pork	豚肉
The dairy products	乳製品
Butter	バター
Cheese	チーズ
Milk	牛乳

32. At the Supermarket / スーパーマーケットで

Yogurt	ヨーグルト
Jam	ジャム
Bread	パン
Eggs	卵
Fish	魚
Seafood	シーフード・魚介
Can	缶詰
Cart	カート
Bag	レジ袋
Basket	かご
Bottle	瓶 / ボトル
Cash register	レジスター
Cashier	レジ係
Customer service	サービスカウンター
Groceries	買い物
How many...?	いくつ・・・？
How many oranges do you buy?	いくつオレンジを買いますか？
How much does it cost?	・・・はいくらですか？
How much do the bananas cost?	バナナはいくらですか？
I want...	私は・・・が欲しいです。/ 私は・・・がしたいです。
I want to buy a bottle of milk	私は牛乳のボトル一つ買いたいです。
I would like...	・・・がしたいのですが。/・・・が欲しいのですが。
I would like a bag of tomatoes	トマト一袋欲しいのですが。
Where is the lettuce?	レタスはどこにありますか？
It's on aisle one	1番売り場にあります
Where are the cans of vegetables?	野菜の缶詰はどこですか？
They are on aisle five	5番売り場にあります。

33. At the Restaurant /
レストランで

Waiter / waitress	ウェイター / ウェイトレス
Breakfast	朝食
Lunch	昼食
Dinner	夕食
To eat	食べる
To drink	飲む
To eat breakfast	朝食を取る
The menu	メニュー
Appetizer	前菜
Salad	サラダ
Soup	スープ
Main course	メインディッシュ
Pasta	パスタ
Rice	米
French fries	ポテトフライ
Mashed potatoes	マッシュポテト
Baked potatoes	ローストポテト
Barbecue	バーベキュー、網焼き
Fried chicken	フライドチキン
Steak	ビフテキ

33. At the Restaurant / レストランで

Dessert	デザート
Beverages	飲み物
Coffee	コーヒー
Tea	茶
Soda	炭酸飲料
Lemonade	レモネード
Orange juice	オレンジジュース
Alcoholic drinks	アルコール飲料
Beer	ビール
Wine	ワイン
Check	お会計・勘定
Tip	チップ
How may I help you?	何か御用でしょうか？
What would you like to order?	ご注文はお決まりですか？
May I have the menu, please?	メニューを見せてください
Could I get more water, please?	お水をもっと持ってきてくれませんか？
My order is wrong	これは注文したものではありません。
The service here is wonderful!	ここのサービスはすばらしい！
The food is delicious!	料理はとても美味しい！
The check, please	お勘定、お願いします
The tip is included	チップ込みです。

34. The Office /
オフィス

Book	本
Calculator	電卓
Computer	パソコン
Desk	(事務) 机
Fax machine	Fax機
File	関係文書
File cabinet	ファイルキャビネット
Folder	ファイル
Keyboard	キーボード
Monitor	モニター
Mouse	マウス
Notebook	ノート
Pad	スケッチブック
Paper	紙、書類
Pen	ボールペン
Printer	印刷機
Ruler	定規
Scissors	鋏
Screen	ディスプレー / スクリーン
Stapler	ホチキス
Telephone	電話
My computer is broken	私のパソコンは壊れた
There is no paper in the printer	印刷機に紙がありません
We need to buy more folders	もっとファイルを買わないといけません。
We don't have a copy machine	私たちはコピー機を持っていません。

35. Jobs and Positions / 職業と地位

Accountant	会計士
Architect	建築家
Artist	芸術家 / アーチスト
Chef	シェフ
Clerk	従業員
Cook	料理人
Doctor	医者
Engineer	技術者・エンジニア
Gardener	庭師 / 園芸家
Graphic designer	グラフィックデザイナー
Lawyer	弁護士
Nurse	看護師
Physician	医者
Salesperson	店員
Secretary	秘書
Security guard	警備員・ガードマン
Taxi driver	タクシー運転手
Teacher	教師
Technician	技術者
Tourist guide	ツアーガイド
Travel agent	旅行代理業者

36. Job Interview /
就職面接

Apply for a job	職を求める
Duty	仕事
Experience	経験
Last name	苗字
First name	名前
Full time job	正社員
Part time job	準社員
Résumé	履歴書
Skill	能力、資格
Work	働く/仕事

37. The Transportation /
交通手段

Airplane	飛行機
Bicycle	自転車
Bus	バス
Car	自動車
Helicopter	ヘリコプター
Metro	地下鉄
Motorcycle	バイク
Train	電車
Truck	トラック

38. The Traffic / 交通

Bus stop	バス停
Crosswalk	横断歩道
Freeway, highway	高速道路
Gas station	ガソリンスタンド
Intersection	交差点
Lane	車線
No outlet	袋小路
One way	一方通行
Pedestrian	歩行者
Speed	速度
Stop sign	一時停止
To get in	乗り込む、乗る
To get off	降車する、降りる
Toll	料金所 / 通行料
Traffic light	信号
Train station	駅
Two way	片側一車線
U-turn	Uターン
Yield	道を譲る
I get in the car	（私は）車に乗ります
I get off the car	（私は）車から降ります
We wait for the train	（私たちは）電車を待ちます

39. The Car /
自動車

Accelerator	アクセル
Battery	バッテリー
Hood	ボンネット
Brake	ブレーキ
Clutch	クラッチ
Engine	エンジン、モーター
Fender	バンパー
Gear box	ギアボックス
Headlight	ライト
Rear view mirror	バックミラー
Make	銘柄 / ブランド
Model	モデル / 機種
Radiator	ラジエーター
Steering wheel	ハンドル
Seat	座席
Tire	タイヤ
Trunk	トランク
Wheel	車輪
Windshield	フロントガラス
Windshield wipers	ワイパー
The car is broken	車は壊れています
I have a flat tire	タイヤの空気圧が下がっています
I need a new battery	(私は) 新しいバッテリーが必要です
What year is the car?	この車は何年産ですか？
What make is the car?	車はどこのですか？ / 車はどこのブランドですか？
What model is the car?	車は何モデルですか？ / 車は何の機種ですか？
How many miles does the car have?	この車の走行距離は何キロですか？

40. Phone Conversations / 電話での会話

Call	電話する、電話をかける
Dial	ダイヤルする
Directory	電話帳
Directory Assistance	案内
Extension	内線番号
Hold on, please	切らずにそのままでお待ちください。
I'd like to speak to...	・・・と話したいのですが。
I'll put you through	伝言しておきます。
I'll transfer your call	おつなぎします
I'm calling about ...	~（用事）でお電話しました
Just a minute	少々お待ちください
Leave a message	メッセージを残す
Let me see...	・・・を見せてください
Phone	電話をかける
Phone number	電話番号
Ring	鳴る
Speak	話す
Speaking	彼 / 彼女は話す
Take a message	メッセージを受け取る
Talk	話す
This is...	私は ~ です
Who's calling?	どちら様ですか？

41. At the Post Office /
郵便局で

Air mail	航空便
Counter	カウンター
Envelope	封筒
Letter	手紙
Mail	郵便物
Parcel	小包
Postcard	はがき
Postman, mailman	郵便配達人
Stamp	郵便切手
To send	発送する
To deliver	渡す
Delivery	配達
To pick up	引き取る
Address	住所
I want to send a letter	（私は）手紙を出したいです
I would like to pick up a parcel	（私は）荷物を引き取りたいのですが。
How much do the stamps cost?	切手はいくらですか？
Do you sell postcards?	絵葉書はありますか？

42. At the Bank / 銀行で

Account	口座
ATM	ATM
Bank statement	取引履歴
Bank teller	窓口係
Cash	現金
Checkbook	小切手帳
Checking account	当座預金
Credit card	クレジットカード
Debit card	デビッドカード
Deposit slip	預金カード
Savings account	貯蓄預金、普通預金
To deposit	預ける
To save	貯蓄する
To transfer	移動させる
To withdraw	引き出す
Transactions	商取引
Withdrawal slip	受領証
I want to make a deposit	預金したいのです
Do you have a savings account?	あなたは普通預金（貯蓄預金）をもっていますか？
I have a checking account	（私は）当座預金を持っています
What is your credit card number?	クレジット番号はなんですか？
I don't have an ATM card	（私は）キャッシュカードを持っていません。
Where are the deposit slips?	振込用紙はどこですか？

43. At the Airport /
空港で

English	Japanese
Arrival	到着
Concourse	通路
Customs	税関
Departure	出発
Destination	目的地
Entrance	入口
Exit	出口
First class	ファーストクラス
Flight	便 / フライト
Gate	ゲート
Immigrations office	入国管理事務所
Luggage	荷物
Passport	パスポート
Restrooms	トイレ
Suitcase	スーツケース
To arrive	到着する
To depart	出発する
To travel	旅行する
Trip	旅行
Where are you traveling?	どこに旅行しますか？
May I have your ticket, please?	乗車券を拝見できますか？
I need you passport, please	パスポートを拝見できますか？
My flight number is ...	私の航空便番号は・・・
Where is gate number ...?	・・・番ゲートはどこですか？
The flight is delayed	この便は遅れています。
The flight is on time	この便は定刻どおりです

44. At the Hotel /
ホテルで

Double room	ツインルーム
Single room	シングルルーム
Bell desk	コンセルジュ
Bellman	ボタン
Elevator	エレベーター
Reception	受付
Receptionist	受付係
Reservation	予約
Stairway	階段
Swimming pool	プール
Tours desk	旅行案内所
Valet parking	駐車場サービス
To check-in	手続きをする
To check-out	ホテルの料金を払う
I would like to make a reservation	予約をしたいのですが
I want a single room	シングルルームを一つお願いします
I would like to check-in	手続きをしたいです

45. The Clothes /
衣服

Bathing suit	バスローブ
Belt	ベルト
Blouse	ブラウス
Coat	コート
Dress	ドレス
Gloves	手袋
Hat	帽子
Jacket	ジャケット
Pants	ズボン
Purse	財布
Scarf	マフラー
Shirt	シャツ
Shoes	靴
Shorts	半ズボン
Skirt	スカート
Socks	ストッキング
Suit	スーツ
Suitcase	スーツケース
The size	サイズ
Small	小
Medium	中
Large	大
Big sizes	大きいサイズ

46. At the Shopping Center / ショッピングモール

Department store	売り場
Ladies	婦人
Men	紳士
Juniors	若者
Kids	子供
Ladies' department	婦人売り場
Jewelry	宝石
Fitting room	試着室
Elevator	エレベーター
Escalator	エスカレーター
How may I help you?	何かお困りですか？
I'm looking for ...	私は～を探しています
I'm just looking	見ているだけです
Where is the fitting room?	試着室はどこですか？
It fits well	私にぴったりです
It doesn't fit well	私には合いません
May I pay here?	ここで払えますか？
I want to exchange this	これを取り替えたいです
I want to return this	これを返品したいです
I like ...	気に入りました
I like this blouse	このブラウスが気に入りました
I don't like ...	気に入りません
I don't like these pants	このズボンは気に入りません

47. At the Drugstore /
薬局で

Antiseptic	消毒剤
Adhesive bandage	絆創膏
Antibiotic	抗生物質
Aspirin	アスピリン
Bandage	包帯
Cold medicine	風邪薬
Cough syrup	のど用シロップ
Medication	薬
Ointment	クリーム
OTC (Over The Counter) medication	一般医薬品
Painkiller	鎮痛剤
Pills	錠剤
Prescription	処方箋
Tablets	錠剤
Thermometer	体温計
Cotton	綿

48. The Parts of the Body / 体の部分

Ankle	くるぶし
Arm	腕
Back	背中
Buttock	尻、臀部
Calf	ふくらはぎ
Chest	胸
Elbow	ひじ
Feet	足
Finger	手の指
Foot	足（くるぶしから下）
Forearm	前腕
Hand	手
Head	頭
Hip	ヒップ
Knee	膝
Leg	脚
Neck	首
Shoulder	肩
Stomach	胃
Thigh	腿
Toe	足の指
Waist	ウエスト
Wrist	手首

49. Health Problems / 健康障害

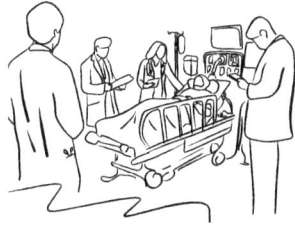

Backache	背中の痛み
Cold	風邪
Fever	熱
Hurt	傷つく
Indigestion	消化不良 / 胃もたれ
Injury	怪我
Pain	痛み
Pulse	脈
Sick	病気
Sneeze	くしゃみ
Sore throat	喉の痛み
Toothache	奥歯の痛み
I have a headache	頭痛がする
I have a stomachache	胃が痛い
I have pain in my knee	ひざが痛い
I hurt my hand	手を怪我した
I've got a cold	風邪を引いている
My foot hurts	足が痛い

50. The Animals / 動物

Bear	熊
Bird	鳥
Cat	猫
Chicken	ひな鳥
Cow	牛
Dog	犬
Duck	アヒル
Elephant	象
Fish	魚
Horse	馬
Lizard	ヤモリ
Lion	ライオン
Monkey	猿
Mouse	ハツカネズミ
Rat	ねずみ
Tiger	トラ

EXERCISE!

Write the Japanese translation.

Keep practicing at:
QuickLanguages.com

1. Greetings / 挨拶

English	Japanese
Hi! / Hello!	こんにちは / やぁ!
Good morning	
Good afternoon	
Good evening / Good night	
How are you doing?	
Fine	
Very well	
Thank you / Thanks	
Thank you very much	
You're welcome	
Fine, thank you	
And you?	
See you	
See you later	
See you tomorrow	
Goodbye	
Bye	

2. Introductions and Courtesy Expressions /
自己紹介と挨拶表現

What is your name?	あなたのお名前は？
My name is ...	
Who are you?	
I am ...	
Who is he / she?	
He is ... / She is ...	
Nice to meet you / Pleased to meet you	
Nice to meet you, too	
It's my pleasure	
Excuse me	
Please	
One moment, please	
Welcome	
Go ahead	
Can you repeat, please?	
I don't understand	
I understand a little	
Can you speak more slowly, please?	
Do you speak Spanish?	
How do you say hello in Spanish?	
What does it mean?	
I speak Spanish a little	

3. Ways to Address to a Person / 人の呼び方

Madam / Ma'am	（既婚）～さん、夫人
Miss	
Ms.	
Mr.	
Mrs.	
Sir	
Dr.	

4. The Articles / 冠詞

The	∅
The car	
The cars	
The house	
The houses	
A	
A car	
A house	
An	
An elephant	
An apple	
Some	
Some cars	
Some houses	

5. The Subject Pronouns /
人称代名詞

I	私
You	
He	
She	
It	
We	
You	
They	

6. The Possessive Adjectives /
属格

My	私の
Your	
His	
Her	
Its	
Our	
Your	
Their	
My car	
Your book	
His TV	
Our house	

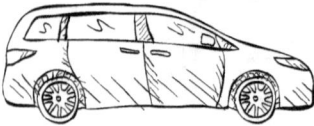

7. The Demonstrative Adjectives / 指示詞

This	この
This book	
This shirt	
These	
These books	
These shirts	
That	
That table	
That car	
Those	
Those tables	
Those cars	

8. The Possessive Pronouns / 所有格

Mine	私の
Yours	
His	
Hers	
Its	
Ours	
Yours	
Theirs	
The car is mine	
The book is yours	
That TV is his	
This house is ours	

9. The Cardinal Numbers /
基本数字

0 / Zero   0   零

1 / One

2 / Two

3 / Three

4 / Four

5 / Five

6 / Six

7 / Seven

8 / Eight

9 / Nine

10 / Ten

11 / Eleven

12 / Twelve

13 / Thirteen

14 / Fourteen

15 / Fifteen

16 / Sixteen

17 / Seventeen

18 / Eighteen

19 / Nineteen

20 / Twenty

21 / Twenty-one

30 / Thirty

40 / Forty

50 / Fifty

60 / Sixty

9. The Cardinal Numbers / 基本数字

70 / Seventy

70　七十

80 / Eighty

90 /Ninety

100 / One hundred

101 / One hundred and one

200 / Two hundred

300 / Three hundred

400 / Four hundred

500 / Five hundred

600 / Six hundred

700 / Seven hundred

800 / Eight hundred

900 /Nine hundred

1,000 / One thousand

10,000 / Ten thousand

100,000 / One hundred thousand

1,000,000 / One million

1,000,000,000 / One billion

Forty-five (45)

One hundred and twenty-eight (128)

One thousand nine hundred and sixty-three (1,963)

Six thousand and thirty-seven (6,037)

Eleven thousand (11,000)

Two hundred and seventy-nine thousand (279,000)

Two million (2,000,000)

10. The Time /
時間

The clock

時計

The watch

What time is it?

It is ...

It is one o'clock (1:00)

It is two o'clock (2:00)

It is three fifteen / It is a quarter past three (3:15)

It is four thirty / It is half past four (4:30)

It is five forty-five / It is a quarter to six (5:45)

It is six fifty / It is ten to seven (6:50)

It is noon (12:00 P. M.)

It is midnight (12:00 A. M.)

In the morning

In the afternoon

In the evening

At night

At what time is ...?

At what time is the concert?

At ...

At 7:10 P.M. (seven ten in the evening)

11. The Days of the Week / 曜日

Monday	月曜日
Tuesday	
Wednesday	
Thursday	
Friday	
Saturday	
Sunday	
What day is today?	

12. The Months of the Year / 月

January	一月
February	
March	
April	
May	
June	
July	
August	
September	
October	
November	
December	
What is today's date?	

13. The Weather /
気候

English	Japanese
Sunny	晴れ
Cloudy	
Rainy	
Humid	
Dry	
Cold	
Warm	
Hot	
Rain	
Snow	
How is the weather today?	
It's nice	
It's sunny	
It's cold in winter	
It's raining	
It's snowing	
I am cold	

14. The Seasons / 季節

Spring	春
Summer	
Fall	
Winter	

15. The Colors / 色

Yellow	黄色
Red	
Blue	
Green	
Orange	
Brown	
Pink	
Purple	
Black	
White	
Gray	
Light	
Dark	
Light green	
Orange book	
Brown shoes	
My blouse is white	
What color is...?	
What is your favorite color?	

16. The Parts of the Face /
顔の部分

頬

Cheek

Chin

Ear

Eye

Forehead

Hair

Lips

Mouth

Nose

Skin

Teeth

Tooth

Blond / Blonde

Brown

Gray

Red hair

Long

Short

Straight

Curly

John is blond

Karen has long hair

He has green eyes

Her eyes are blue

His eyes are big and brown

17. Essential Verbs /
基本動詞

Be	~ である
Go	
Come	
Have	
Get	
Help	
Love	
Like	
Want	
Buy	
Sell	
Read	
Write	
Drink	
Eat	
Open	
Close	
Look at	
Look for	
Find	
Start	
Stop	
Pull	

17. Essential Verbs /
基本動詞

押す

Push	
Send	
Receive	
Turn on	
Turn off	
Listen to	
Speak	
Do	
Drive	
Feel	
Know	
Leave	
Live	
Make	
Meet	
Need	
Pay	
Play	
Remember	
Repeat	
Say	
Sit	
Sleep	

17. Essential Verbs /
基本動詞

Study	勉強する
Take	
Think	
Understand	
Wait	
Watch	
There is	
There are	
I am tall	
You are short	
He is thin	
We are big	
They are intelligent	
I am at home	
You are at school	
We are at the store	
I get a prize	
I go to the movies	
I have a nice car	
I listen to the music	
I watch TV.	
I like this book	
There are ten children in the park	

18. Interrogative Words /
疑問文

How many …?	いくつの（複数形）・・・？
How much…?	
How …?	
What …?	
When …?	
Where …?	
Which …?	
Who …?	
Whose …?	
Whom …? / To whom …?	
Why …?	
Because …	

19. Linking Words /
接続詞

And	・・・と
But	
Or	
Either … or	
Neither … nor	
Yes	
No	
So	
While	

20. The Prepositions/
前置詞

About	～について
Above	
Across	
At	
Behind	
Below	
Between	
By	
Down	
During	
For	
From	
In	
In front of	
Into	

20. The Prepositions/
前置詞

Near	近くに
Next to	
Of	
On	
Out	
Over	
Per	
Through	
To	
Under	
Up	
With	
Without	
The cat is in the box	
The vase is on the table	
Somebody is at the door	

21. Giving Directions / 道案内

English	Japanese
At the corner	角に
Far	
Near	
Go straight ahead	
Left	
Right	
Turn left	
Turn right	
Go straight one block	
After the traffic light, turn right	
How can I get to ...?	
Where is the ...?	
Where is the church?	
The museum is next to the shopping center	
The drugstore is in front of the building	
The supermarket is near the park	

22. The Ordinal Numbers / 序数

First	最初の、第1の
Second	
Third	
Fourth	
Fifth	
Sixth	
Seventh	
Eighth	
Ninth	
Tenth	
Eleventh	
Twelfth	
Twentieth	
Thirtieth	
The first building	
The second floor	

23. Countries, Nationalities, and Languages / 国・国籍・言語

Brazil (Country)	ブラジル（国）
Brazilian (Nationality)	
Portuguese (Language)	
Colombia	
Colombian	
Spanish	
China	
Chinese	
Chinese	
England	
English	
English	
France	
French	
French	
Germany	
German	
German	
Italy	

23. Countries, Nationalities, and Languages /
国・国籍・言語

Italian   イタリア人

Italian

Japan

Japanese

Japanese

Mexico

Mexican

Spanish

Spain

Spanish

Spanish

United States of America (U.S.A.)

American

English

Where are you from?

I am from Brazil

I am Brazilian

I speak Portuguese

I am not from Italy

24. Indefinite Pronouns / 不定代名詞

誰か（疑問）、誰も（否定）

Anybody	
Anything	
Nobody	
Nothing	
Somebody	
Something	
Everybody	
Everything	
Is anybody home?	
I don't want anything	
Nothing happened	
Somebody is in the living room	
Everything is ready	

25. The Emotions /
感情

怒った

Angry

Bored

Confident

Confused

Embarrassed

Excited

Happy

Nervous

Proud

Sad

Scared

Shy

Surprised

Worried

I am happy

He is sad

They are surprised

Are you excited?

I am not bored

She is not nervous

Everybody is confident

26. Adverbs /
副詞

A few	少しの
A little	
A lot	
After	
Again	
Ago	
Also	
Always	
Before	
Enough	
Everyday	
Exactly	
Finally	
First	
Here	
Late	
Later	
Never	
Next	
Now	

26. Adverbs /
副詞

しょっちゅう

Often

Once

Only

Outside

Really

Right here

Right now

Since

Slowly

Sometimes

Soon

Still

Then

There

Today

Tomorrow

Tonight

Too

Usually

27. Auxiliary Verbs / 助動詞

・・・できる

Can	
Could	
Did	
Do	
Does	
Have to	
May	
Must	
Should	
Will	
Would	
Can you go to the movies?	
Could I have change?	
Did you work at the drugstore?	
I did not (didn't) work at the drugstore	
Do you work at the drugstore?	
I do not (don't) work at the drugstore	
Does he read the newspaper?	
He does not (doesn't) read the newspaper	
I have to do my homework	
May I help you?	
You must turn left now	
You should go to the doctor	
I will work tomorrow	
I would like a glass of wine	

28. Expressions / 表現

それで良い

All right	
Come in	
Come here, please	
Don't worry!	
For example	
Good luck!	
Great idea!	
Have a nice day!	
Help yourself!	
Here you are	
Hurry up!	
I agree	
I disagree	
I don't care	
I don't know	
I'm coming!	
I'm afraid...	
It's a deal!	
Keep well!	
Let me think	
Let's go!	
Right now	
Sounds good!	
Sure	
Take a seat	
Take care!	

29. The Family /
家族

Father	父
Mother	
Son	
Daughter	
Brother	
Sister	
Grandfather	
Grandmother	
Uncle	
Aunt	
Cousin	
Nephew	
Niece	
Husband	
Wife	
Boyfriend	
Girlfriend	
In-laws	
Father in-law	
Mother in-law	
Brother in-law	
Sister in-law	
Step father	
Step mother	
Step brother	
Step sister	
Who is he?	
He is my brother	

30. The House /
家

応接間

Living room

Door

Window

Sofa

Lamp

Dining room

Table

Chair

Kitchen

Stove

Oven

Fridge

Microwave

Bedroom

Bed

Nightstand

Vanity

Chest of drawers

Closet

Bathroom

Mirror

Sink

Toilet

Bathtub

Laundry room

Driveway

Where is the living room?

The door is big

The stove is small

The kitchen is beautiful

31. The City /
街

Block	街区 / ブロック
Building	
Church	
Movie theater	
Museum	
Park	
Drugstore	
Restaurant	
Shopping center	
Store	
Street	
Supermarket	

32. At the Supermarket /
スーパーマーケットで

食品

The food

The fruits

Apple

Banana

Cherry

Grapes

Orange

Strawberry

The vegetables

Beans

Carrot

Cauliflower

Lettuce

Onion

Pepper

Potato

Tomato

The meats

Beef

Chicken

Turkey

Ham

Pork

The dairy products

Butter

Cheese

Milk

32. At the Supermarket / スーパーマーケットで

Yogurt	ヨーグルト
Jam	
Bread	
Eggs	
Fish	
Seafood	
Can	
Cart	
Bag	
Basket	
Bottle	
Cash register	
Cashier	
Customer service	
Groceries	
How many...?	
How many oranges do you buy?	
How much does it cost?	
How much do the bananas cost?	
I want...	
I want to buy a bottle of milk	
I would like...	
I would like a bag of tomatoes	
Where is the lettuce?	
It's on aisle one	
Where are the cans of vegetables?	
They are on aisle five	

33. At the Restaurant /
レストランで

English	Japanese
Waiter / waitress	ウェイター / ウェイトレス
Breakfast	
Lunch	
Dinner	
To eat	
To drink	
To eat breakfast	
The menu	
Appetizer	
Salad	
Soup	
Main course	
Pasta	
Rice	
French fries	
Mashed potatoes	
Baked potatoes	
Barbecue	
Fried chicken	
Steak	

33. At the Restaurant /
レストランで

Dessert	デザート
Beverages	
Coffee	
Tea	
Soda	
Lemonade	
Orange juice	
Alcoholic drinks	
Beer	
Wine	
Check	
Tip	
How may I help you?	
What would you like to order?	
May I have the menu, please?	
Could I get more water, please?	
My order is wrong	
The service here is wonderful!	
The food is delicious!	
The check, please	
The tip is included	

34. The Office /
オフィス

Book

Calculator

Computer

Desk

Fax machine

File

File cabinet

Folder

Keyboard

Monitor

Mouse

Notebook

Pad

Paper

Pen

Printer

Ruler

Scissors

Screen

Stapler

Telephone

My computer is broken

There is no paper in the printer

We need to buy more folders

We don't have a copy machine

35. Jobs and Positions / 職業と地位

Accountant	会計士
Architect	
Artist	
Chef	
Clerk	
Cook	
Doctor	
Engineer	
Gardener	
Graphic designer	
Lawyer	
Nurse	
Physician	
Salesperson	
Secretary	
Security guard	
Taxi driver	
Teacher	
Technician	
Tourist guide	
Travel agent	

36. Job Interview /
就職面接

職を求める

Apply for a job

Duty

Experience

Last name

First name

Full time job

Part time job

Résumé

Skill

Work

37. The Transportation /
交通手段

飛行機

Airplane

Bicycle

Bus

Car

Helicopter

Metro

Motorcycle

Train

Truck

38. The Traffic / 交通

Bus stop	バス停
Crosswalk	
Freeway, highway	
Gas station	
Intersection	
Lane	
No outlet	
One way	
Pedestrian	
Speed	
Stop sign	
To get in	
To get off	
Toll	
Traffic light	
Train station	
Two way	
U-turn	
Yield	
I get in the car	
I get off the car	
We wait for the train	

39. The Car /
自動車

Accelerator

Battery

Hood

Brake

Clutch

Engine

Fender

Gear box

Headlight

Rear view mirror

Make

Model

Radiator

Steering wheel

Seat

Tire

Trunk

Wheel

Windshield

Windshield wipers

The car is broken

I have a flat tire

I need a new battery

What year is the car?

What make is the car?

What model is the car?

How many miles does the car have?

アクセル

40. Phone Conversations /
電話での会話

Call	電話する、電話をかける
Dial	
Directory	
Directory Assistance	
Extension	
Hold on, please	
I'd like to speak to...	
I'll put you through	
I'll transfer your call	
I'm calling about ...	
Just a minute	
Leave a message	
Let me see...	
Phone	
Phone number	
Ring	
Speak	
Speaking	
Take a message	
Talk	
This is...	
Who's calling?	

41. At the Post Office /
郵便局で

Air mail	航空便
Counter	
Envelope	
Letter	
Mail	
Parcel	
Postcard	
Postman, mailman	
Stamp	
To send	
To deliver	
Delivery	
To pick up	
Address	
I want to send a letter	
I would like to pick up a parcel	
How much do the stamps cost?	
Do you sell postcards?	

42. At the Bank /
銀行で

Account	口座
ATM	
Bank statement	
Bank teller	
Cash	
Checkbook	
Checking account	
Credit card	
Debit card	
Deposit slip	
Savings account	
To deposit	
To save	
To transfer	
To withdraw	
Transactions	
Withdrawal slip	
I want to make a deposit	
Do you have a savings account?	
I have a checking account	
What is your credit card number?	
I don't have an ATM card	
Where are the deposit slips?	

43. At the Airport /
空港で

Arrival

Concourse

Customs

Departure

Destination

Entrance

Exit

First class

Flight

Gate

Immigrations office

Luggage

Passport

Restrooms

Suitcase

To arrive

To depart

To travel

Trip

Where are you traveling?

May I have your ticket, please?

I need you passport, please

My flight number is ...

Where is gate number ...?

The flight is delayed

The flight is on time

44. At the Hotel / ホテルで

Double room	ツインルーム
Single room	
Bell desk	
Bellman	
Elevator	
Reception	
Receptionist	
Reservation	
Stairway	
Swimming pool	
Tours desk	
Valet parking	
To check-in	
To check-out	
I would like to make a reservation	
I want a single room	
I would like to check-in	

45. The Clothes /
衣服

バスローブ

Bathing suit	
Belt	
Blouse	
Coat	
Dress	
Gloves	
Hat	
Jacket	
Pants	
Purse	
Scarf	
Shirt	
Shoes	
Shorts	
Skirt	
Socks	
Suit	
Suitcase	
The size	
Small	
Medium	
Large	
Big sizes	

46. At the Shopping Center / ショッピングモール

Department store	売り場
Ladies	
Men	
Juniors	
Kids	
Ladies' department	
Jewelry	
Fitting room	
Elevator	
Escalator	
How may I help you?	
I'm looking for ...	
I'm just looking	
Where is the fitting room?	
It fits well	
It doesn't fit well	
May I pay here?	
I want to exchange this	
I want to return this	
I like ...	
I like this blouse	
I don't like ...	
I don't like these pants	

47. At the Drugstore /
薬局で

Antiseptic	消毒剤
Adhesive bandage	
Antibiotic	
Aspirin	
Bandage	
Cold medicine	
Cough syrup	
Medication	
Ointment	
OTC (Over The Counter) medication	
Painkiller	
Pills	
Prescription	
Tablets	
Thermometer	
Cotton	

48. The Parts of the Body /
体の部分

English	Japanese
Ankle	くるぶし
Arm	
Back	
Buttock	
Calf	
Chest	
Elbow	
Feet	
Finger	
Foot	
Forearm	
Hand	
Head	
Hip	
Knee	
Leg	
Neck	
Shoulder	
Stomach	
Thigh	
Toe	
Waist	
Wrist	

49. Health Problems /
健康障害

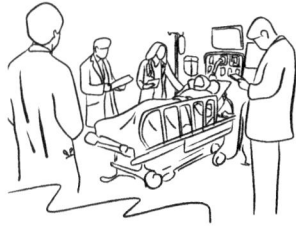

背中の痛み

Backache

Cold

Fever

Hurt

Indigestion

Injury

Pain

Pulse

Sick

Sneeze

Sore throat

Toothache

I have a headache

I have a stomachache

I have pain in my knee

I hurt my hand

I've got a cold

My foot hurts

50. The Animals /
動物

Bear	熊
Bird	
Cat	
Chicken	
Cow	
Dog	
Duck	
Elephant	
Fish	
Horse	
Lizard	
Lion	
Monkey	
Mouse	
Rat	
Tiger	

EXERCISE!

Write the English translation.

Keep practicing at:
QuickLanguages.com

1. Greetings / 挨拶

こんにちは / やぁ！	Hi! / Hello!
おはようございます	
こんにちは / やぁ！	
こんばんは	
元気ですか？ / ご機嫌いかがで すか？	
元気です	
とても元気です	
ありがとう	
どうもありがとう	
どういたしまして	
元気です、ありがとう	
君は（のほうは元気）？	
またね	
また後で	
また明日	
さようなら	
バイバイ、じゃぁね	

2. Introductions and Courtesy Expressions /
自己紹介と挨拶表現

What is your name?

あなたのお名前は？
私の名前は・・・
どなたですか？
私は・・・
彼 (el)/彼女(ella) は誰ですか？
彼(el) / 彼女(ella) は・・・
お会いできて光栄です
こちらこそ、お会いできて光栄です
光栄です
すみません
お願いします / ～して下さい
少しお待ちください
ようこそ
お入りください
もう一度、繰り返して下さい
分かりません
少し理解できます
ゆっくり話してくれませんか？
スペイン語を話しますか？
ハロー(hello)はスペイン語で何と言いますか？
これは何という意味ですか？
私は少しスペイン語を話します。

3. Ways to Address to a Person / 人の呼び方

（既婚）～さん、夫人	Madam / Ma'am
（未婚）～さん、～嬢	
～さん	
（男性）～さん、～氏	
（既婚）女性	
男性	
博士	

4. The Articles / 冠詞

∅	The
自動車	
自動車（複数形）	
家	
家（複数形）	
∅	
自動車	
家	
∅	
象	
リンゴ	
いくつかの	
自動車（複数形）	
家（複数形）	

5. The Subject Pronouns / 人称代名詞

私
君 / あなた
彼
彼女
彼たち、彼ら
私たち
あなたたち
彼ら / 彼女ら

6. The Possessive Adjectives / 属格

私の　　　　　　　　My
君の
彼の
彼女の
彼らの
私たちの
君たちの
彼たちの　/　彼女たちの
私の自動車
君の本
彼のテレビ
私たちの家

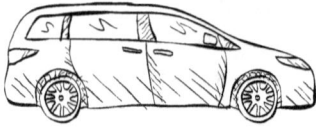

7. The Demonstrative Adjectives / 指示詞

この	This
この本	
このシャツ	
これらの	
これらの本	
これらのシャツ	
その	
そのテーブル	
その自動車	
それらの	
それらのテーブル	
それらの自動車	

8. The Possessive Pronouns / 所有格

私の	Mine
君の	
彼の	
彼女の	
彼の	
私たちの	
君たちの	
彼 / 彼女たちの	
自動車は私のです	
本は君のです	
そのテレビは彼女のです	
この家は私たちのです	

9. The Cardinal Numbers / 基本数字

0	零
1	一
2	二
3	三
4	四
5	五
6	六
7	七
8	八
9	九
10	十
11	十一
12	十二
13	十三
14	十四
15	十五
16	十六
17	十七
18	十八
19	十九
20	二十
21	二十一
30	三十
40	四十
50	五十
60	六十

0 / Zero

1. 2. 3. 4.
5. 6. 7. 8.
9. 0.

9. The Cardinal Numbers /
基本数字

70	七十	*70 / Seventy*
80	八十	
90	九十	
100	百	
101	百一	
200	二百	
300	三百	
400	四百	
500	五百	
600	六百	
700	七百	
800	八百	
900	九百	
1000	千	
10000	一万	
100000	十万	
1000000	百万	
1000000000	十億	
45	四十五	
128	百二十八	
1963	千九百六十三	
6037	六千三十七	
11000	一万千	
279000	二十七万九千	
2000000	二百万	

10. The Time /
時間

The clock

時計

腕時計

何時ですか？

・・・時です

1時です

2時です

3時15分です

4時30分です / 4時半です

5時45分です / 6時15分前です

6時50分です / 7時10分前です

正午です

真夜中 / 午前零時

午前中に

午後に

夜に

夜に

・・・は何時ですか？

コンサートは何時ですか？

・・・時に

夜7時に

11. The Days of the Week / 曜日

月曜日	Monday
火曜日	
水曜日	
木曜日	
金曜日	
土曜日	
日曜日	
今日は何曜日ですか？	

12. The Months of the Year / 月

一月	January
二月	
三月	
四月	
五月	
六月	
七月	
八月	
九月	
十月	
十一月	
十二月	
今日は何日ですか？	

13. The Weather /
気候

晴れ　　　　　　　　　　Sunny

曇り

雨がちの

じめじめした

乾燥した

寒い

暑い

暑い

雨

雪

今日の天気はどうですか？

いい天気です

晴れています

冬は寒いです

雨が降っています

雪が降っています

（私は）寒いです

14. The Seasons / 季節

春	*Spring*
夏	
秋	
冬	

15. The Colors / 色

Yellow

黄色
赤
青
緑
オレンジ色
茶色
ピンク色
赤紫色
黒
白
灰色
明るい
暗い
明るい緑（黄緑）
オレンジ色の本
茶色い靴
私のブラウスは白です
・・・は何色ですか？
君の好きな色は何ですか？

16. The Parts of the Face / 顔の部分

Cheek

頬

顎

耳

目

おでこ

髪

唇

口

鼻

皮膚

歯（複数形）

歯

金髪の

栗毛の

白髪の

赤毛の

長い

短い

直毛の

巻毛の

ジョンは金髪です

カレンは髪が長いです

彼は緑目です

彼の目は青いです

彼の目は大きくて茶色です

17. Essential Verbs / 基本動詞

Japanese	English
〜である	Be
行く	
来る	
持つ	
達成する、獲得する	
助ける、手伝う	
愛する	
気に入る	
欲する；望む、願う	
買う	
売る	
読む	
書く	
飲む	
食べる	
開く、開ける	
閉める、閉じる	
見る	
探す	
見つける	
始める	
止める	
引っ張る	

17. Essential Verbs /
基本動詞

Push

押す

送る

受け取る

点火する ; スイッチを入れる

消す

聞く

話す

する

操る ; 操作する

感じる

知っている

出る

生きる ; 住む

準備する

知り合う

必要とする

払う

遊ぶ

思い出す / 覚えている

繰り返す

言う

座る

寝る

17. Essential Verbs /
基本動詞

Japanese	English
勉強する	Study
取る、つかむ	
考える	
理解する	
待つ	
観察する	
ある	
ある	
私は（背が）高いです	
君は（背が）小さいです	
彼は痩せています	
私たちは大きいです	
彼らは頭が良いです	
私は家に居ます	
君は学校にいます	
私たちはお店にいます	
私は賞を取ります	
私は映画館に行きます	
私は素敵な自動車を持っています	
私は音楽を聞きます	
私はテレビを観ます	
私はこの本が好きです	
公園に10人の子供がいます	

18. Interrogative Words /
疑問文

いくつの（複数形）・・・？   How many ...?
いくつの（単数形）・・・？
どのように？
何？
いつ？
どこで？
どれ？
誰？
誰の？
誰に？
なぜ？
なぜなら・・・

19. Linking Words /
接続詞

・・・と   And
しかし、でも・・・
または
・・・か・・・か
・・・も・・・もない
はい
いいえ
それでは
・・・している間

20. The Prepositions / 前置詞

~ について	About
~ の上に	
~ の前に	
~ に	
~ の後ろに	
~ の下に	
~ の間に	
~ で〔交通手段〕	
下方に	
~ の間に〔時間・期間〕	
~ のために	
~ から	
~ の中に	
~ の正面に	
中に	

20. The Prepositions /
前置詞

近くに	Near
～の隣に	
～の	
～の上に	
外に	
～の上に	
～で、～のゆえに	
～を通して	
～の方へ	
下に	
上に	
～と一緒に	
～なしに	
箱の中に猫がいます	
テーブルの上に花瓶があります	
玄関に誰か居ます	

21. Giving Directions / 道案内

角に	At the corner
遠くに	
近くに	
まっすぐ進んでください	
左	
右	
左に曲がる	
右に曲がる	
1街区（ブロック）まっすぐ進んでください	
信号の後で右に曲がる	
・・・へはどのように行けばいいですか？	
・・・はどこですか？	
教会はどこですか？	
美術館はショッピングセンターの隣です。	
薬局はビルの前です。	
スーパーマーケットは公園の近くです。	

22. The Ordinal Numbers / 序数

First

最初の、第1の	
2番目の、第2の	
3番目の、第3の	
4番目の、第4の	
5番目の、第5の	
6番目の、第6の	
7番目の、第7の	
8番目の、第8の	
9番目の、第9の	
10番目の、第10の	
11番目の、第11の	
12番目の、第12の	
20番目の；20分の1	
30番目の；30分の1	
最初の建物	
1 階	

23. Countries, Nationalities, and Languages / 国・国籍・言語

ブラジル (国)	Brazil (Country)
ブラジル人 (国籍)	
ポルトガル語 (言語)	
コロンビア	
コロンビア人	
スペイン語	
中国	
中国人	
中国語	
イギリス	
イギリス人	
英語	
フランス	
フランス人	
フランス語	
ドイツ	
ドイツ人	
ドイツ語	
イタリア	

23. Countries, Nationalities, and Languages /
国・国籍・言語

イタリア人	Italian
イタリア語	
日本	
日本人	
日本語	
メキシコ	
メキシコ人	
スペイン語	
スペイン	
スペイン人	
スペイン語	
アメリカ合衆国	
アメリカ人	
英語	
どこの出身ですか？	
私はブラジル出身です。	
私はブラジル人です。	
私はポルトガル語を話します。	
私はイタリア出身ではありません。	

24. Indefinite Pronouns / 不定代名詞

誰か（疑問）、誰も（否定）	Anybody
何か（疑問）、何も（否定）	
誰も	
何も	
誰か（肯定）	
何か（肯定）	
全部（複数形）、すべて	
全部、すべて	
どなたか家に居ますか？	
何もいらない	
なんでもない	
応接間に誰かいる	
準備万端	

25. The Emotions /
感情

Angry

怒った

つまらない

自信を持った

混乱した

恥じている

熱狂した

満足した

緊張した

誇り高い

悲しい

怖がらせた

内気な

驚いた

心配させた

（私は）満足しています

彼は悲しんでいます

彼らは驚いています

あなたは興奮(熱狂)していますか？

（私は）退屈していません

彼女は緊張していません

すべての人は自信を持っています

26. Adverbs /
副詞

日本語	English
少しの	A few
わずかな	
たくさんの	
後で	
もう一度	
後ろへ	
・・・もまた	
いつも	
前に、以前に	
十分に	
毎日	
正確に	
最後に	
まず最初に	
ここ	
遅く、遅れて	
もっと遅く	
決して（・・・ない）	
次の、近い	
今	

26. Adverbs /
副詞

しょっちゅう

often

一回

・・・だけ、ただ・・・

外へ

現実に、本当に

ちょうど此処

今すぐに

・・・から

ゆっくりと

時々、たまに

すぐに

まだ（・・・ない）

後で

あちらの方へ

今日

明日

今晩

・・・もまた

通常、ふつう

27. Auxiliary Verbs / 助動詞

・・・できる	Can
・・・してくれませんか	
・・・できた	
する	
する	
・・・しなければならない	
・・・しても良い	
・・・しなければならない	
・・・したほうが良い	
∅	
∅	
映画を観にいける？	
両替していただけますか？	
（君は）薬局で働いていた？	
（私は）薬局では働いていませんでした。	
（君は）薬局で働いている？	
（私は）薬局では働いていません。	
彼は新聞を読みますか？	
彼は新聞を読みません。	
（私は）自分の仕事をしなければなりません。	
何かお手伝いできますか？	
（君は）今、左に曲がるべきだ。	
（君は）医者に行くべきだ。	
（私は）明日働きます。	
（私は）ワイン一杯いただけますか？	

28. Expressions /
表現

All right

それで良い

どうぞ

こちらに来てください。

心配いらないよ！

例えば・・・

幸運を！

グッド・アイディア！

良い一日を（過ごしてください）！

どうぞご自由に！ / セルフサービスです！

どうぞ

急いで！

賛同する、賛成する

私は反対です

私はどちらでもいいです

知りません

今、行きます！

・・・ではないかと心配する

約束したぞ！ / 話しは決まった！

ごきげんよう

考えさせてください

さあ！ / さあ行こう！

たった今 / 現在

いいね

確かに

お座りください

気をつけて！

29. The Family / 家族

父	Father
母	
息子	
娘	
兄弟	
姉妹	
祖父	
祖母	
伯父・叔父	
伯母・叔母	
いとこ	
甥	
姪	
夫	
妻	
彼氏 / 新郎	
彼女 / 新婦	
義理の家族	
義父・舅	
義母・姑	
義兄・義弟	
義姉・義妹	
継父	
継母	
異父（異母）の兄弟	
異父（異母）の姉妹	
彼は誰ですか？	
彼は私の兄（弟）です。	

30. The House /
家

Living room

応接間
ドア・扉
窓
ソファ
ランプ
食堂
テーブル / 机
椅子
台所 / キッチン
ストーブ
オーブン
冷蔵庫
電子レンジ
寝室
ベッド
ナイトテーブル
鏡台
整理だんす
クローゼット
浴室
鏡
洗面台 / 洗面所
水洗トイレ
浴槽
コインランドリー
駐車場
応接室はどこですか？
ドアは大きいです。
ストーブは小さいです。
キッチンは素敵です。

31. The City / 街

街区 / ブロック	Block
ビル / 建物	
教会	
映画館	
美術館 / 博物館	
公園	
薬局	
レストラン	
ショッピングセンター	
店	
道	
スーパーマーケット	

32. At the Supermarket /
スーパーマーケットで

The food

食品
果物
リンゴ
バナナ
さくらんぼ
ブドウ
オレンジ
苺
野菜
インゲン豆
人参
カリフラワー
レタス
玉ねぎ
ピーマン
ジャガイモ
トマト
肉
牛肉
鶏肉
七面鳥
生ハム
豚肉
乳製品
バター
チーズ
牛乳

32. At the Supermarket / スーパーマーケットで

ヨーグルト	Yogurt
ジャム	
パン	
卵	
魚	
シーフード・魚介	
缶詰	
カート	
レジ袋	
かご	
瓶 / ボトル	
レジスター	
レジ係	
サービスカウンター	
買い物	
いくつ・・・？	
いくつオレンジを買いますか？	
・・・はいくらですか？	
バナナはいくらですか？	
私は・・・が欲しいです。/ 私は・・・がしたいです。	
私は牛乳のボトル一つ買いたいです。	
・・・がしたいのですが。/ ・・・が欲しいのですが。	
トマト一袋欲しいのですが。	
レタスはどこにありますか？	
1番売り場にあります	
野菜の缶詰はどこですか？	
5番売り場にあります。	

33. At the Restaurant /
レストランで

ウェイター / ウェイトレス	Waiter / waitress
朝食	
昼食	
夕食	
食べる	
飲む	
朝食を取る	
メニュー	
前菜	
サラダ	
スープ	
メインディッシュ	
パスタ	
米	
ポテトフライ	
マッシュポテト	
ローストポテト	
バーベキュー、網焼き	
フライドチキン	
ビフテキ	

33. At the Restaurant / レストランで

デザート	Dessert
飲み物	
コーヒー	
茶	
炭酸飲料	
レモネード	
オレンジジュース	
アルコール飲料	
ビール	
ワイン	
お会計・勘定	
チップ	
何か御用でしょうか？	
ご注文はお決まりですか？	
メニューを見せてください	
お水をもっと持ってきてくれませんか？	
これは注文したものではありません。	
ここのサービスはすばらしい！	
料理はとても美味しい！	
お勘定、お願いします	
チップ込みです。	

34. The Office /
オフィス

Book

本

電卓

パソコン

（事務）机

Fax機

関係文書

ファイルキャビネット

ファイル

キーボード

モニター

マウス

ノート

スケッチブック

紙、書類

ボールペン

印刷機

定規

鋏

ディスプレー / スクリーン

ホチキス

電話

私のパソコンは壊れた

印刷機に紙がありません

もっとファイルを買わないといけま
せん。

私たちはコピー機を持っていませ
ん。

35. Jobs and Positions /
職業と地位

会計士	Accountant
建築家	
芸術家 / アーチスト	
シェフ	
従業員	
料理人	
医者	
技術者・エンジニア	
庭師 / 園芸家	
グラフィックデザイナー	
弁護士	
看護師	
医者	
店員	
秘書	
警備員・ガードマン	
タクシー運転手	
教師	
技術者	
ツアーガイド	
旅行代理業者	

36. Job Interview /
就職面接

Apply for a job

職を求める

仕事

経験

苗字

名前

正社員

準社員

履歴書

能力、資格

働く/仕事

37. The Transportation /
交通手段

飛行機

Airplane

自転車

バス

自動車

ヘリコプター

地下鉄

バイク

電車

トラック

38. The Traffic /
交通

日本語	English
バス停	Bus stop
横断歩道	
高速道路	
ガソリンスタンド	
交差点	
車線	
袋小路	
一方通行	
歩行者	
速度	
一時停止	
乗り込む、乗る	
降車する、降りる	
料金所 / 通行料	
信号	
駅	
片側一車線	
Uターン	
道を譲る	
(私は)車に乗ります	
(私は)車から降ります	
(私たちは)電車を待ちます	

39. The Car /
自動車

Accelerator

アクセル

バッテリー

ボンネット

ブレーキ

クラッチ

エンジン、モーター

バンパー

ギアボックス

ライト

バックミラー

銘柄 / ブランド

モデル / 機種

ラジエーター

ハンドル

座席

タイヤ

トランク

車輪

フロントガラス

ワイパー

車は壊れています

タイヤの空気圧が下がっています

（私は）新しいバッテリーが必要です

この車は何年産ですか？

車はどこのですか？ / 車はどこのブランドですか？

車は何モデルですか？ / 車は何の機種ですか？

この車の走行距離は何キロですか？

40. Phone Conversations / 電話での会話

電話する、電話をかける	Call
ダイヤルする	
電話帳	
案内	
内線番号	
切らずにそのままでお待ちください。	
・・・と話したいのですが。	
伝言しておきます。	
おつなぎします	
～（用事）でお電話しました	
少々お待ちください	
メッセージを残す	
・・・を見せてください	
電話をかける	
電話番号	
鳴る	
話す	
彼／彼女は話す	
メッセージを受け取る	
話す	
私は～です	
どちら様ですか？	

41. At the Post Office /
郵便局で

航空便

カウンター

封筒

手紙

郵便物

小包

はがき

郵便配達人

郵便切手

発送する

渡す

配達

引き取る

住所

（私は）手紙を出したいです

（私は）荷物を引き取りたいの
ですが。

切手はいくらですか？

絵葉書はありますか？

42. At the Bank / 銀行で

口座	Account
ATM	
取引履歴	
窓口係	
現金	
小切手帳	
当座預金	
クレジットカード	
デビッドカード	
預金カード	
貯蓄預金、普通預金	
預ける	
貯蓄する	
移動させる	
引き出す	
商取引	
受領証	
預金したいのです	
あなたは普通預金（貯蓄預金）をもっていますか？	
（私は）当座預金を持っています	
クレジット番号はなんですか？	
（私は）キャッシュカードを持っていません。	
振込用紙はどこですか？	

43. At the Airport /
空港で

到着

通路

税関

出発

目的地

入口

出口

ファーストクラス

便 / フライト

ゲート

入国管理事務所

荷物

パスポート

トイレ

スーツケース

到着する

出発する

旅行する

旅行

どこに旅行しますか？

乗車券を拝見できますか？

パスポートを拝見できますか？

私の航空便番号は・・・

・・・番ゲートはどこですか？

この便は遅れています。

この便は定刻どおりです

44. At the Hotel / ホテルで

Japanese	English
ツインルーム	Double room
シングルルーム	
コンセルジュ	
ボタン	
エレベーター	
受付	
受付係	
予約	
階段	
プール	
旅行案内所	
駐車場サービス	
手続きをする	
ホテルの料金を払う	
予約をしたいのですが	
シングルルームを一つお願いします	
手続きをしたいです	

45. The Clothes /
衣服

Bathing suit

バスローブ

ベルト

ブラウス

コート

ドレス

手袋

帽子

ジャケット

ズボン

財布

マフラー

シャツ

靴

半ズボン

スカート

ストッキング

スーツ

スーツケース

サイズ

小

中

大

大きいサイズ

46. At the Shopping Center / ショッピングモール

売り場	Department store
婦人	
紳士	
若者	
子供	
婦人売り場	
宝石	
試着室	
エレベーター	
エスカレーター	
何かお困りですか？	
私は～を探しています	
見ているだけです	
試着室はどこですか？	
私にぴったりです	
私には合いません	
ここで払えますか？	
これを取り替えたいです	
これを返品したいです	
気に入りました	
このブラウスが気に入りました	
気に入りません	
このズボンは気に入りません	

47. At the Drugstore /
薬局で

消毒剤   Antiseptic

絆創膏

抗生物質

アスピリン

包帯

風邪薬

のど用シロップ

薬

クリーム

一般医薬品

鎮痛剤

錠剤

処方箋

錠剤

体温計

綿

48. The Parts of the Body /
体の部分

くるぶし	Ankle
腕	
背中	
尻、臀部	
ふくらはぎ	
胸	
ひじ	
足	
手の指	
足（くるぶしから下）	
前腕	
手	
頭	
ヒップ	
膝	
脚	
首	
肩	
胃	
腿	
足の指	
ウエスト	
手首	

49. Health Problems /
健康障害

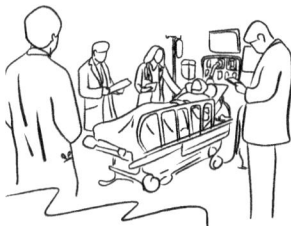

Backache

背中の痛み

風邪

熱

傷つく

消化不良 / 胃もたれ

怪我

痛み

脈

病気

くしゃみ

喉の痛み

奥歯の痛み

頭痛がする

胃が痛い

ひざが痛い

手を怪我した

風邪を引いている

足が痛い

50. The Animals /
動物

熊	Bear
鳥	
猫	
ひな鳥	
牛	
犬	
アヒル	
象	
魚	
馬	
ヤモリ	
ライオン	
猿	
ハツカネズミ	
ねずみ	
トラ	

QUICK LANGUAGES

MULTI-LANGUAGE PHRASEBOOK COLLECTION

SPEAK ANY LANGUAGE NOW!

QUICK LANGUAGES PHRASEBOOK COLLECTION
AVAILABLE TITLES

1. ENGLISH-SPANISH & SPANISH-ENGLISH
2. ENGLISH-ITALIAN & ITALIAN-ENGLISH
3. ENGLISH-FRENCH & FRENCH-ENGLISH
4. ENGLISH-GERMAN & GERMAN-ENGLISH
5. ENGLISH-PORTUGUESE & PORTUGUESE-ENGLISH
6. ENGLISH-CHINESE & CHINESE-ENGLISH
7. ENGLISH-ARABIC & ARABIC-ENGLISH
8. ENGLISH-JAPANESE & JAPANESE-ENGLISH
9. ENGLISH-KOREAN & KOREAN-ENGLISH
10. ENGLISH-RUSSIAN & RUSSIAN-ENGLISH
11. ENGLISH-TURKISH & TURKISH-ENGLISH

GET THE AUDIOVISUAL AND
INTERACTIVE CONTENT AT
QuickLanguages.com

www.ingramcontent.com/pod-product-compliance
Lightning Source LLC
LaVergne TN
LVHW021452080426
835509LV00018B/2255